Rigby Literacy
Collections 2
Middle Primary

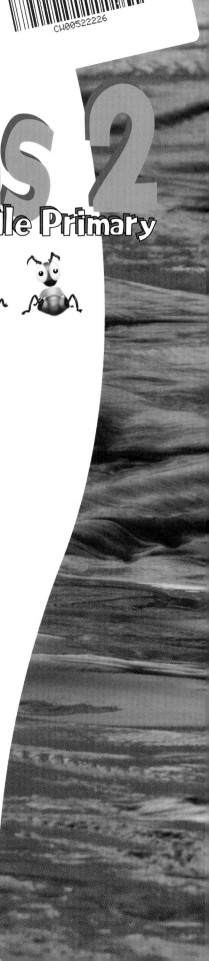

Rigby

Contents

THE River's Journey

Rob Morrison

Far inland, storm clouds gather around mountain peaks. Lightning flashes, thunder rumbles and rain begins to fall. The rain has begun its long journey to the sea. It will travel by way of a river.

Rivers start as little streams. The streams join together to form a river. A river cuts its own path to the sea. As it flows, it picks up earth and carries it away. This process is called water erosion. Erosion can eventually wear away great mountains.

The river erodes a channel through the earth. This eroded channel is called a river bed. A river bed can dry out in summer, but will fill up again when the winter rains fall.

Sometimes, snow that falls in the mountains does not melt, but forms a river of ice called a glacier. Glaciers flow like rivers, but they flow very slowly. Most glaciers flow less than one metre each day. Where a glacier melts, it forms a river of water.

A glacier.

Water is soft, but over millions of years it can wear rocks away. Many rivers run through valleys that they have formed. The flowing ice of a glacier makes valleys in the form of a "U". The flowing water of rivers cuts valleys shaped like a "V".

River valleys are sometimes called gorges or canyons. They can be very deep and wide. The Grand Canyon in America is twenty-nine kilometres across at its widest part. It is 349 kilometres long and more than one and a half kilometres deep.

Other forces can shape a river, too. An earthquake can move the earth, making a rocky step in a river. When the water flows over the step, it makes a waterfall. In time, the water will erode the rocky step away.

The Grand Canyon.

People build dams in rivers. A dam may be used to store water to drive hydro-electric power stations, or to store water for the irrigation of crops. Many dams are reservoirs which store water for people in cities to use.

A dam storing water for a hydro-electric power station.

Most rivers run to the sea, but they do not run straight. Some rivers split into two, or join with other rivers. Some rivers bend around mountains in their path. Some rivers run into lakes or swamps, and flow out the other side. Some rivers wander in large loops that grow bigger each year.

A loop can get so big that the river cuts a new channel past it. The loop then becomes a billabong or a backwater. Backwaters are quiet places where many birds come to breed.

A backwater.

An estuary.

In time, the river will reach the sea. An estuary forms where the river and the sea meet. Fresh water from the river pours into the sea. Tides push salt water from the sea into the river mouth. Plants and animals of estuaries can live in fresh water and salt water. Estuaries are often places where fish breed.

Once river water has reached the sea, its journey is not over. The sun's heat makes water vapour from the surface of the sea. The winds blow the water vapour far inland. Reaching the cold mountains, the water vapour forms clouds. Lightning flashes, thunder roars, water falls from the clouds as rain. The river begins its journey again.

"Gummies" Grab Victory!

Nick Dean

Gumlit Primary School produced the upset of the season by beating the favourite, Highbrow Primary School, in the semi-final of the District Soccer Cup. The "Gummies", as Gumlit Primary are known, displayed flair and determination as they sneaked to victory, winning 2–1.

During most of the first half, not one shot was on target, in fact, it was difficult to imagine that a place in next week's Cup Final was at stake. However, just before half-time, Highbrow played some great soccer, and Gareth Baddley found the net. The score: 1–nil. Highbrow went into the break, full of confidence.

But a competitive will to win kept the Gummies in the game. In the second half, Gummie's Alvin Ling, in an inspired manner, raced down the field and scored a convincing goal. The score was now one goal each.

Alvin Ling about to score a goal.

The last two minutes of the match were thrilling. The Gummies needed to win in order to reach the final. Again, Gareth Baddley, from Highbrow, went for a goal, but "Gummie Goalie" Steven Howe was equal to the task, and produced an awesome save.

And then, in a matter of seconds, Gummie's Carlos de Silva received a pass and raced down the field. But the excitement didn't stop there!

Goalie Steven Howe in action.

Highbrow's Duncan "Brutus" Forest made an illegal tackle, dragging Carlos to the ground. Duncan was given a yellow card and the Gummies sniffed victory.

Carlos de Silva smashed the ball into the back of the net and the game was sealed.

**Gumlit Primary 2,
Highbrow Primary 1.**

The Gummies go into next week's Cup Final full of confidence.

On the Right Track

Stephen Gard

A map is a picture that helps us to find places and to understand things. There are many different types of maps, depending on the information that you need.

A road map shows where roads go and where they join other roads. It names the towns that roads pass through, and tells how far it is from one place to another.

Families use a road map on a holiday trip. Taxi drivers and couriers use a road map to find the right place when driving people or taking parcels to destinations. A road map helps police, ambulance drivers and firefighters to reach an emergency quickly.

A street directory map.

These firefighters are checking their destination on a map.

A relief map.

A relief map shows the height of hills, the depth of valleys, the area of forests and the width of lakes and rivers. Engineers use relief maps to build dams, bridges or a new freeway.

Plans are maps, too. They show how to make something. An architect draws plans for a new house. The plans tell a plumber where the pipes should go, and an electrician can see where to put the wires. Diagrams are plans that show how something works, such as a computer or an engine.

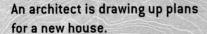

An architect is drawing up plans for a new house.

Aeroplane pilots use charts to check their course through the sky. Ships' captains and navigators also use charts to plan their course over the sea. Charts have grid lines drawn on them. Navigators can use a compass, radio beams and signals from satellites to discover which grid lines their ship or aeroplane is near.

A navigator using a map to discover where her ship is in the sea.

A farmer checking the sky for rain.

A weather map is a picture of the Earth taken by a satellite. It shows clouds, rain, hot and cold places, and which way the wind is blowing. Pilots, farmers and fishermen often use weather maps to tell them if the weather will change or if a storm is coming. They can then prepare for these changes.

Maps are very important in our daily lives. They certainly keep us on the right track!

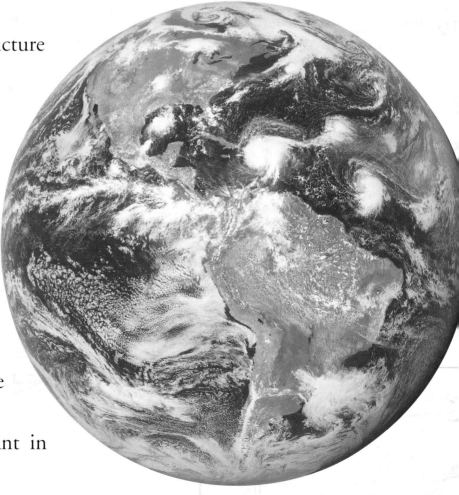
A world weather map.

SUCKED INTO THE SKY

38 Die as Tornadoes Blow Residents From Their Homes

Special report by Martin Merzer, Phil Long and Lori Rosza

A tornado that tore through Florida yesterday was so strong that people were tossed hundreds of metres through the air. One person was lifted and dumped in the middle of the Florida Turnpike, normally one of the busiest highways in the state.

The destruction caused by the tornado in Kissimmee, Florida.

Attacking during the night, the worst swarm of tornadoes in Florida's history is thought to have killed at least thirty-eight people. Ten more are still missing. Rescue teams and their dogs worked through the night, probing the wreckage for survivors.

The twisters, some with winds in excess of 400 kilometres per hour, sucked people out of their homes, spinning them into the air. One teenager was blown out of a window and landed 45 metres away in a cow pasture, and lived to tell the tale.

The winds injured more than 250 people. Hospitals were battling to cope with the numbers needing help. Thousands of homes and businesses were destroyed or damaged, and thousands of people lost cars and boats.

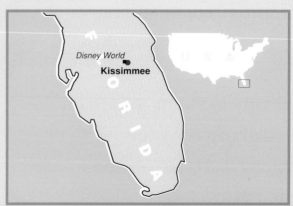

J eff Hall, a county fire chief, said, "We have patients who are alive after being blown several hundred yards from their homes. There were people flying through the air, crossing canals. It was a pretty nasty sight."

Meteorologists counted at least six, and possibly as many as ten, monstrous tornadoes.

(Daily Telegraph: 25/2/98.)

Caught in a Tempest

Timothy, an old man, and Phillip, a young boy who is blind, have been marooned on a deserted island since their ship sank. They are preparing for a hurricane that is approaching the island. They are sheltering in a hut, but, as a back-up plan, Timothy has lashed a tin box and a water keg to a palm tree that is on higher ground.

At sunset, with the air heavy and hot, Timothy described the sky to me. He said it was flaming red and that there were thin veils of high clouds. It was so still over our cay that we could hear nothing but the rustling of the lizards.

Just before dark. Timothy said, "'Twon't be long now, Phill-eep."

We felt a light breeze that began to ripple the smooth sea. Timothy said he saw an arc of very black clouds to the west.

They looked as if they were beginning to join the higher clouds.

It was well after dark when the first drops of rain spattered the hut, and with them, the wind turned cool. When it gusted, the rain hit the hut like handfuls of gravel.

Then the wind began to blow steadily, and Timothy went out of the hut to look up at the sky. He shouted, "Dey boilin' ovah now, Phill-eep. 'Tis hurrican', to be sure."

We could hear the surf beginning to crash as the wind drove waves before it, and Timothy ducked back inside to stand in the opening of the hut, his big body stretched so he could hang on to the overhead frame, keeping the hut erect as long as possible.

I felt movement around my legs and feet. Things were slithering. I screamed to Timothy who shouted back, "B'nothin' but d'lil' lizard, comin' high ground."

Rain was now slashing into the hut, and the wind was reaching a steady howl. The crash of the surf sounded closer; I wondered if it was already beginning to push up towards our hill. The rain was icy, and I was wet, head to foot. I was shivering, but more from the thought of the sea rolling over us than from the sudden cold.

In a moment, there was a splintering sound, and Timothy dropped down beside me, covering my body with his. Our hut had blown away.

There was no sound now except the roar of the storm. Even the sound of the wind was being beaten down by the wildness of the sea. The rain was hitting my back like thousands of hard berries blown from air guns.

We stayed flat on the ground for almost two hours, taking the storm's punishment, barely able to breathe in the driving rain. Then Timothy shouted hoarsely, "To d'palm."

The sea was beginning to reach for our hilltop, climbing the forty feet with raging whitecaps. Timothy dragged me towards the palm.

Standing with his back to the storm, Timothy put my arms through the loops of rope, and then roped himself, behind me, to the tree.

Soon, I felt water around my ankles. Then it washed to my knees. It would go back and then crash against us again. Timothy was taking the full blows of the storm, sheltering me with his body. When the water receded, it would tug at us, and Timothy's strength would fight against it. I could feel the steel in his arms as the water tried to suck us away.

We must have been against the palm for almost an hour when suddenly the wind died down and the rain became gentle. Timothy panted, "D'eye! We can relax a bit till d'odder side o' d' tempis' hit us."

from *The Cay*
by Theodore Taylor

A Lesson Learnt

Rat has taken his new friend Mole for a ride along the river in his boat.

The afternoon sun was getting low as the Rat sculled gently homewards in a dreamy mood, murmuring poetry-things over to himself, and not paying much attention to Mole. But the Mole was very full of lunch, and self-satisfaction, and pride, and already quite at home in a boat (so he thought) and was getting a bit restless besides: and presently he said, "Ratty! Please, *I* want to row now!"

The Rat shook his head with a smile. "Not yet, my young friend," he said—"wait till you've had a few lessons. It's not so easy as it looks."

The Mole was quiet for a minute or two. But he began to feel more and more jealous of Rat, sculling so strongly and so easily along, and his pride began to whisper that he could do it every bit as well. He jumped up and seized the sculls, so suddenly, that the Rat, who was gazing out over the water, was taken by surprise and fell backwards off his seat with his legs in the air for the second time, while the triumphant Mole took his place and grabbed the sculls with entire confidence.

"Stop it, you *silly* ass!" cried the Rat, from the bottom of the boat. "You can't do it! You'll have us over!"

The Mole flung his sculls back with a flourish, and made a great dig at the water. He missed the water altogether, his legs flew up above his head, and he found himself lying on top of the prostrate Rat. Greatly alarmed, he made a grab at the side of the boat, and the next moment—Sploosh!

Over went the boat, and he found himself struggling in the river.

O my, how cold the water was, and O, how *very* wet it felt. How it sang in his ears as he went down, down, down! How bright and welcome the sun looked as he rose to the surface coughing and spluttering! How black was his despair when he felt himself sinking again!

Then a firm paw gripped him by the back of his neck. It was the Rat, and he was laughing—the Mole could *feel* him laughing, right down his arm and through his paw, and so into his—the Mole's—neck.

The Rat got hold of a scull and shoved it under the Mole's arm; then he did the same by the other side of him and, swimming behind, propelled the helpless animal to shore, hauled him out, and set him down on the bank, a squashy, pulpy lump of misery.

When the Rat had rubbed him down a bit, and wrung some of the wet out of him, he said, "Now then, old fellow! Trot up and down the towing path as hard as you can, till you're warm and dry again…"

* * *

When all was ready for a start once more, the Mole, limp and dejected, took his seat in the stern of the boat; and as they set off, he said in a low voice, broken with emotion, "Ratty, my generous friend! I am very sorry indeed for my foolish and ungrateful conduct… Indeed, I have been a complete ass, and I know it. Will you overlook it this once and forgive me, and let things go on as before?"

"That's all right, bless you!" replied the Rat cheerily. "What's a little wet to a Water Rat? I'm more in the water than out of it most days. Don't you think any more about it…"

The Mole was so touched by his kind manner of speaking that he could find no voice to answer him; and he had to brush away a tear or two with the back of his paw.

from *The Wind in the Willows* by Kenneth Grahame

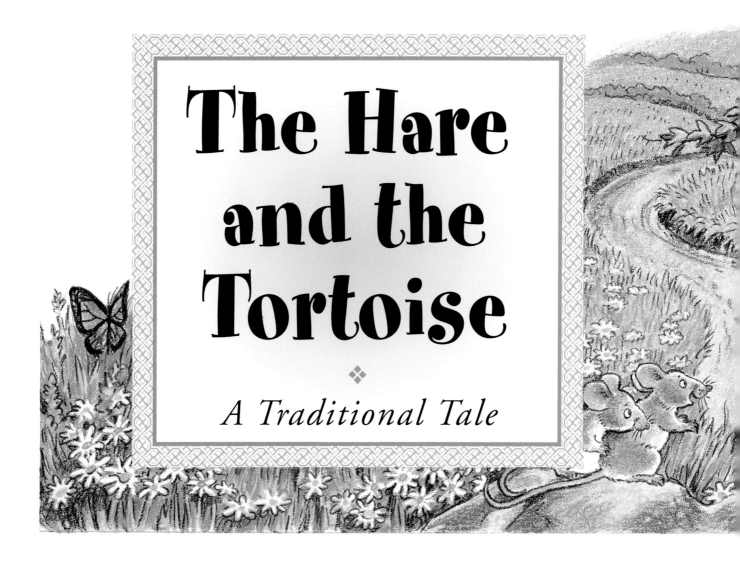

The Hare and the Tortoise

A Traditional Tale

A hare was once teasing a tortoise about being so slow. "You're as slow as a wet week," he said. "Any animal could race you and win. You couldn't run out of sight in a month."

The tortoise was feeling quite hurt by this. He hit back bravely, saying, "Don't you make fun of me! I bet I could beat you anyway."

"Whaaat! Beat me! Not in a million years!" boasted the hare.

"All right," said the tortoise, "let's have a race and see who wins."

"Are you serious?" said the hare.

"Why not?" said the tortoise.

This is going to be easy, thought the hare, and so he agreed to race.

They decided that the fox should act as starter and judge.

"Ready...Set...Go!" said the fox, and the race began.

The hare set off at a great rate and very soon the tortoise could just see him disappearing into the distance. It was quite a warm day, and before long, the hare began to feel hot and tired. He decided he had plenty of time to have a rest and still beat the slow tortoise, so he lay down on the soft grass and fell asleep.

Meanwhile, the tortoise kept plodding along at his steady pace, not stopping at all. Eventually he overtook the sleeping hare, and still he kept plodding on.

When the hare finally woke up, he ran as fast as he could to the finish line, but when he got there he found that the tortoise had already finished.

"*Slow and steady* can beat fast any day," said the tortoise with pride.

The Ants at the Olympics

At last year's Jungle Olympics,
the Ants were completely outclassed.
In fact, from an entry of sixty-two teams,
the Ants came their usual last.

They didn't win one single medal.
Not that that's a surprise.
The reason was not lack of trying,
but more their unfortunate size.

While the cheetahs won most of the sprinting
and the hippos won putting the shot,
the Ants tried sprinting but couldn't,
and tried to put but could not.

It was sad for the Ants 'cause they're sloggers.
They turn out for every event.
With their shorts and their bright orange tee-shirts,
their athletes are proud they are sent.

They came last at the high jump and hurdles,
which they say they'd have won, but they fell.
They came last in the four hundred metres
and last in the swimming as well.

They came last in the long-distance running,
though they say they might have come first.
And they might if the other sixty-one teams
hadn't put in a finishing burst.

But each year they turn up regardless.
They're popular in the parade.
The other teams whistle and cheer them,
aware of the journey they've made.

For the Jungle Olympics in August,
they have to set off New Year's Day.
They didn't arrive the year before last.
They set off but went the wrong way.

So long as they try there's a reason.
After all, it's only a sport.
They'll be back next year to bring up the rear,
and that's an encouraging thought.

Richard Digance

GRAN, CAN YOU RAP?

GRAN, CAN YOU RAP?

GRAN, CAN YOU RAP?

Gran was in her chair she was taking a nap
  When I tapped her on the shoulder to see if
    she could rap.
Gran, can you rap? Can you rap? Can you, Gran?
And she opened one eye and she said to me, man,
I'm the best rapping Gran this world's ever seen
I'm a tip-top, slip-slap, rap-rap queen.

And she rose from her chair in the corner of the room
And she started to rap with a bim-bam-boom,
And she rolled up her eyes and she rolled round her head
And as she rolled by this is what she said,
I'm the best rapping Gran this world's ever seen
I'm a nip-nap, yip-yap, rap-rap queen.

Then she rapped past my dad and she rapped past my mother,
She rapped past me and my little baby brother.
She rapped her arms narrow she rapped her arms wide,
She rapped through the door and she rapped outside.
She's the best rapping Gran this world's ever seen
She's a drip-drop, trip-trap, rap-rap queen.

She rapped down the garden she rapped down the street,
The neighbours all cheered and they tapped their feet.
She rapped through the traffic lights as they turned red.
As she rapped round the corner this is what she said,
I'm the best rapping Gran this world's ever seen,
I'm a flip-flop, hip-hop, rap-rap queen.

She rapped down the lane she rapped up the hill,
And as she disappeared she was rapping still.
I could hear Gran's voice saying, listen, man,
Listen to the rapping of the rap-rap Gran.
I'm the best rapping Gran this world's ever seen.
I'm a —
Tip-top, slip-slap,
Nip-nap, yip-yap,
Hip-hop, trip-trap,
Touch yer cap,
Take a nap,
Happy, happy, happy, happy,
Rap-rap queen.

Jack Ousbey

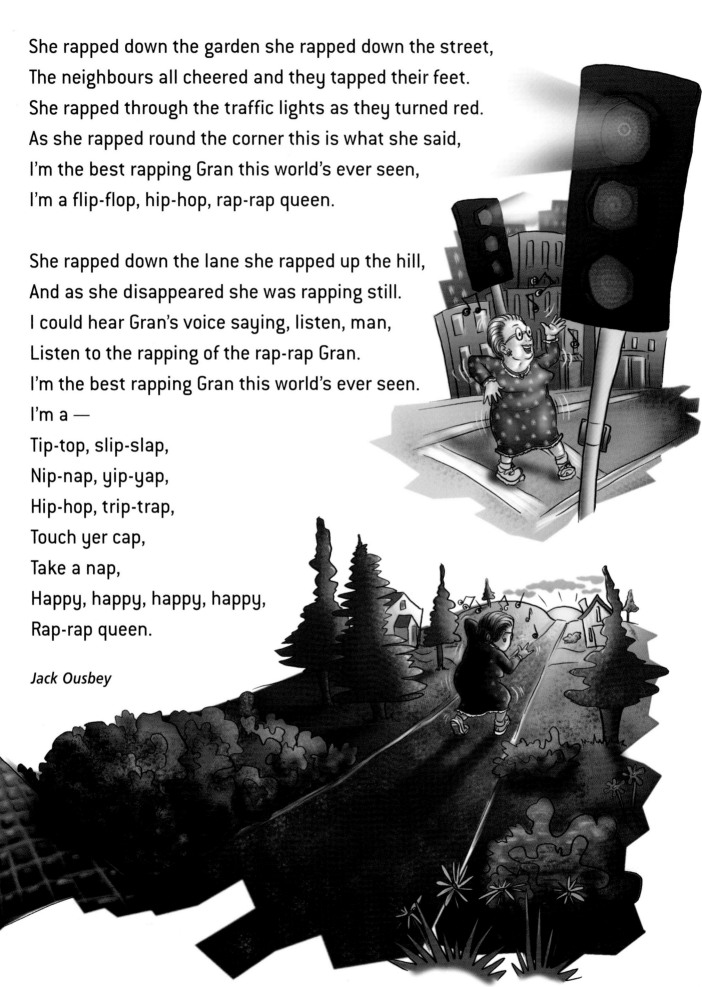

Uncle Ollie's farm

Kerri Lane

"What would you like to do tomorrow?" Aunt Kate asked.

Becky looked at her brother. Tom flopped back in the chair.

"You must do something special on your first day!" Uncle Ollie boomed.

"Can we come with you?"

"You'd have to get up very, very early, Becky. While it's still dark."

Aunt Kate smiled. "Uncle Ollie's fixing a fence down near the river. You could swim and have a picnic. But he's leaving far too early."

"We could come a bit later," Tom suggested.

"I suppose I could leave a map so you'll find me." said Uncle Ollie.

Tom cheered. "That would be great!"

The next morning, as Aunt Kate rushed out the door, she said "Uncle Ollie's map is on the table. I'll meet you at the river later, but I have to see a sick cow."

Tom and Becky walked outside into the lovely sunshine. "Let me see the map," said Tom.

"No way. I'm in charge." Becky looked at the map. "This is easy. We just follow these directions through the farm."

"Are you sure?" asked Tom.

Becky nodded. "The first direction says 'Rose'. That'll be the rose garden. There's a line that points straight ahead."

Leading the way, Becky charged off. The perfume from the garden was beautiful. So were the roses. There were red, pink and yellow ones.

"These flowers are gorgeous! Look at that dark red one down the bottom! I'm going to pick just one petal…"

As she plucked the soft feathery petal, a loud screech came from the rose bush.

"That's not a rose! It's the rooster's tail! The cranky rooster!" cried Tom.

"I know that!" snapped Becky. "Run!"

With the rooster snapping at their heels, they headed to the next point on the map. "It's says 'Penny'," Becky puffed. "I'm sure that's the name of the sheep. Remember? The line goes to the left and then straight again."

At the sheep paddock, Tom frowned. "Do we go through the gate or do we turn here?"

"Through it."

"Wait!"

The words came too late. Becky swung back the gate. And then screamed.

There seemed to be hundreds of sheep and lambs running everywhere.

"Grab them!"

Becky turned. "I can't."

Tom dived and missed and landed in a big pile of mud. Little lambs ran in all directions. Becky fell in the feed trough.

The "hundreds" of sheep turned out to be ten—but they made enough noise for a hundred. Finally, Becky and Tom managed to get them all back in their paddock.

Tom sighed. This was a weird map—maybe Uncle Ollie was playing a joke on them. "Where to next?"

"There's a right turn and then it says 'Bill'."

"Bill? What does that mean?"

Becky started walking. "Let's see where it leads…"

The right turn took them to a big paddock. Climbing through the wire fence, they were still wondering what "Bill" meant.

Suddenly Tom knew. The snorting sound was the clue. "Don't turn around—just head straight for that tree and climb as fast as you can."

"Why?"

"Because Bill is the bull!"

Sitting up on a high branch, Becky and Tom looked back below them. Bill the bull didn't seem very angry, but they weren't taking any chances.

They sat and they sat. Finally, they saw Uncle Ollie's old truck. They waved and he drove to the gate.

"We were worried," he said as he helped them down. "Why are you up here?"

"We were scared of Bill."

Uncle Ollie frowned. "Who's Bill?"

"Your bull!" exclaimed Becky.

Uncle Ollie scratched his head. "The bull's name is Clem."

"But the map said to turn right to find Bill."

Becky pulled out the map and Uncle Ollie threw back his head and laughed.

"That's not the map! That's Aunt Kate's family tree. There's your great great-Aunt Rose, and your Aunt Penny and your third cousin Bill."

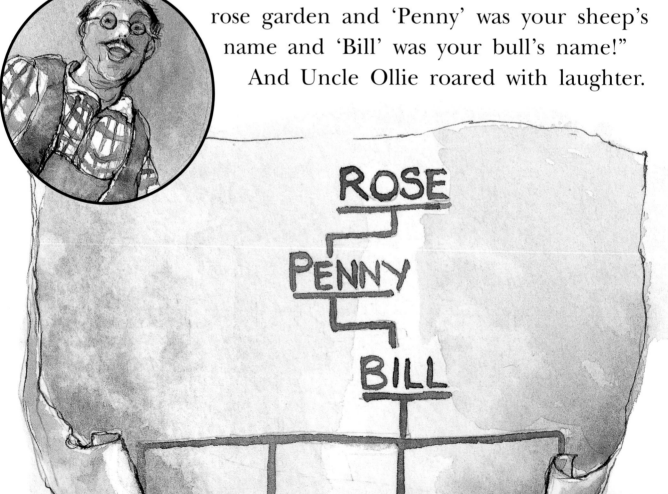

"But I thought the word 'Rose' meant the rose garden and 'Penny' was your sheep's name and 'Bill' was your bull's name!"

And Uncle Ollie roared with laughter.

The Hippopotamus

Behold the hippopotamus!

We laugh at how he looks to us,

And yet in moments dank and grim

I wonder how we look to him.

Peace, peace, thou hippopotamus!

We really look all right to us,

As you no doubt delight the eye

Of other hippopotami.

Ogden Nash

Training
for the Big Day

Edward is a young hippopotamus who is intent on entering the Twenty-Seventh Annual African Hippopotamus Race. Edward's grandfather, Theodore, is training him.

Every morning, when it was still dark and ordinary, hippopotamuses were still asleep, with the sky like velvet and the stars just starting to go out, Edward leapt from his bed, out of his pyjamas and into his bathing trunks. Wasting not a second, looking to neither left nor right, he ran for the river at the end of the garden, and dived in.

Splash!

First he swam eight kilometres down the river, going as fast as he could. Then he flipped over and came all the way back, trying to go even faster. His little bulgy eyes were closed tight—except for an occasional fast look just to make sure he was going in the right direction—while his huge mouth was open one minute, closed the next, sucking up enormous breaths. Over and over went his arms, cleaving a pathway through the water. And with each stroke of an arm, he gave a powerful kick with a leg.

Whoosh! Whoosh!

And no sooner was he back at the garden than he immediately began twenty minutes of vigorous exercises, touching his toes, running on the spot, windmills, press-ups, deep knee bends and two-legged leaps.

"How did it go, Champ?" Edward's father asked him. Ever since Edward started training, his father had taken to calling him "Champ".

"Terrific!" Edward said. "I feel fine."

And how hungry he was after all that exercising. Six eggs! Four glasses of milk!

Ten pieces of toast, each thickly buttered and covered with marmalade.

"Watch that diet, Champ," his father said.

"Quickly, now," said Edward's mother, "It's time for school."

And Edward had just enough time to change into his school clothes, grab his school bag, and run off.

Back he came at twelve o'clock, when school finished for the day, and hippopotamuses went home for lunch and to sleep in the afternoon—a very sensible thing to do when it's hot.

His grandfather allowed Edward only one hour's sleep—most hippopotamuses have three or four—and then training began again.

This time, when Edward dived into the river, his grandfather jumped on to a bicycle, and as Edward swam down the river, his grandfather bicycled along the bank, shouting out instructions through a megaphone.

"Keep your head down! Keep your head down! Use your legs! Use your legs!"

"Push with that left leg! Push with that left leg!" he shouted, his legs flying on the bicycle pedals.

"That'll do! That'll do! Come out! Come out! Take a rest. Whew! You're too fast for me."

Poor old Theodore. It was a long time since he had done anything as strenuous as bicycling up and down a river bank, shouting instructions through a megaphone. He felt a bit wobbly in the legs.

"How's it going, Champ?" said Edward's father.

"Fine!" said Edward. "I feel terrific."

"He's too fast for me," said Edward's grandfather. "I'm out of breath. Just a minute. Lots to do. Lots to do. Lotssssss…"

Edward's grandfather was asleep.

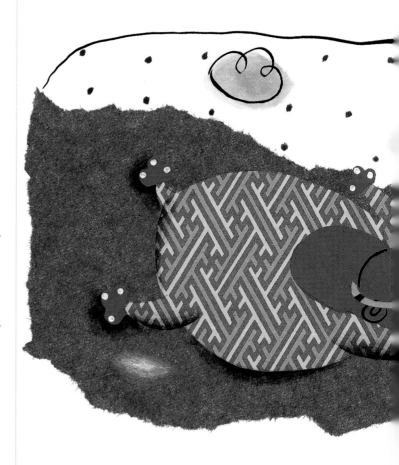

But an hour later he was back again, as keen as ever.

"Now, Edward," he said, "back into the river. This time I'm going to time you with my stop watch. I want you to swim five kilometres, up to that tree, as fast as you can. Ready? On your mark! Go!"

That night when Edward was in bed, fast asleep, Edward's grandfather sat down at the family desk, unscrewed his fountain pen, and, very carefully, wrote a letter to the President of the Twenty-Seventh Annual African Hippopotamus Race.

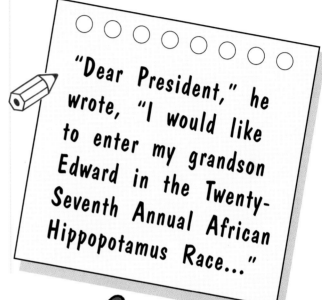

"Dear President," he wrote, "I would like to enter my grandson Edward in the Twenty-Seventh Annual African Hippopotamus Race..."

from *The Twenty-Seventh Annual African Hippopotamus Race* by Morris Lurie

POOR TOM

Rodney Bennett

At the table poor Tom sits
And sees the food go by.
He cannot eat a single bite,
He seems to have no appetite,
And wonders why.

"Since breakfast I have only had
Two pears," he sadly thinks,
"Five biscuits—those with sugared tops—
Eight nuts, and two small ginger pops
Or so by way of drinks;

"Four apples, one small slice of cake,
One strip of liquorice,
Three bull's-eyes and a brandy-ball—
I really do not see at all
Why I should feel like this."

So at the table poor Tom sits
And sees the food go by,
And cannot eat a single bite;
He seems to have no appetite—
And wonders why!

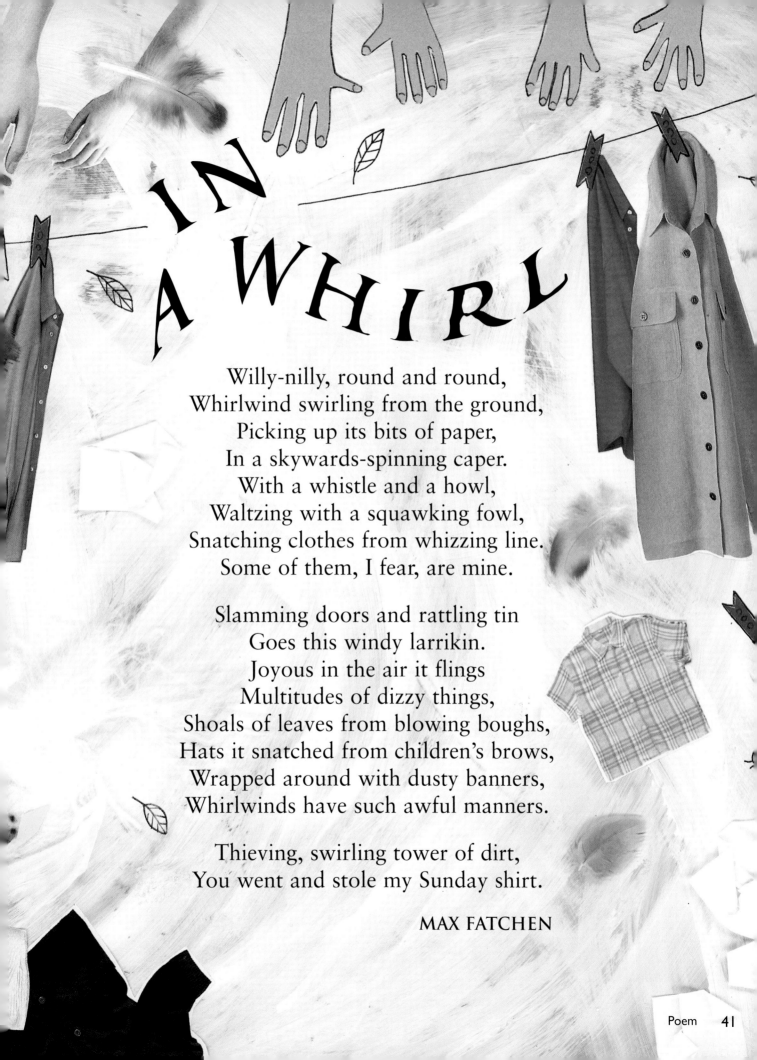

IN A WHIRL

Willy-nilly, round and round,
Whirlwind swirling from the ground,
Picking up its bits of paper,
In a skywards-spinning caper.
With a whistle and a howl,
Waltzing with a squawking fowl,
Snatching clothes from whizzing line.
Some of them, I fear, are mine.

Slamming doors and rattling tin
Goes this windy larrikin.
Joyous in the air it flings
Multitudes of dizzy things,
Shoals of leaves from blowing boughs,
Hats it snatched from children's brows,
Wrapped around with dusty banners,
Whirlwinds have such awful manners.

Thieving, swirling tower of dirt,
You went and stole my Sunday shirt.

MAX FATCHEN

My Earthquake Scrapbook

Helen Chapman

On Tuesday, 17 October 1989, at 5.04 p.m. an earthquake hit my city of San Francisco. It lasted about fifteen seconds. Mum, my brother Tim and I were at home. When it was over, we didn't know if Dad was safe. That was the worse thing about the Loma Prieta earthquake.

At Candlestick Park

Sixty-two thousand fans, including my dad, were at a baseball game. Dad said there was a loud noise. When the earthquake hit, the ground shook and lamp-posts swayed. Concrete slabs on the upper deck of the stadium moved apart—some people saw the sky on the other side! Then the slabs moved back together. No-one panicked because the shaking stopped so quickly. In fact, Dad said that everyone clapped! I couldn't understand why. Dad said this was because it seemed normal to be in San Francisco watching a ball game and have an earthquake! Grown-ups are weird!

Out and About

The roads were busy with peak hour traffic when the earthquake began. Some drivers felt their vehicles jiggling. Bricks and glass from buildings dropped onto some vehicles. Other vehicles and their drivers faced even greater danger. One freeway rocked so badly that parts of it slammed together and columns split.

Some vehicles were crushed. Traffic lights went out. Cars, buses and cable cars stopped. Over thirty trains stopped in the subway. This left thousands of people stranded in dark tunnels and underground stations.

People ran out of shaking offices and into the streets. Having had such a fright made strangers talk to each other like friends.

Fact File

Every earthquake has a centre or epicentre. Loma Prieta's was 15 km north-east of Santa Cruz and 97 km south of San Francisco. It occurred along a fault line known as the San Andreas Fault. The fault looks like a long valley.

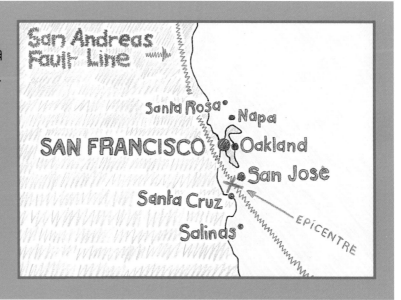

At Home

Before the earthquake began, I had turned on the TV to see if I could see Dad at the baseball game. Then, the picture on the screen rocked and just as a voice said, "We're having an earth..." the TV screen went black! At the same time, the house shook and the floor wobbled. I knew I should "Duck, Cover and Hold", but I couldn't move. I was too scared. Mum dragged me under the table. Things crashed to the floor and plaster and dust flew everywhere.

When the house stopped shaking, there was rubble all around us. We were trapped!

Search and Rescue

From under the table, we smelt smoke and heard sirens. Suddenly, there was a big THWACK! A firefighter broke through the door with an axe! A police officer came through as well, and found us. She said our house wasn't on fire, but it had huge cracks. It wasn't safe because it could fall down any minute. I thought it already had!

We were homeless, along with a lot of other people. The police officer took us to our local school which was set up as a rescue centre. Dad was already there. When he saw us, we all hugged and cried. We were given blankets, torches and water. That night, we slept in the school gymnasium.

Fact File

The strength of an earthquake is measured by the Richter scale. A reading of less than 2 is a small quake, a reading of 8 or higher is a big quake. The Loma Prieta earthquake was 7.1.

Fact File

Homeless people: 12,000
Homes destroyed: 400
Homes damaged: 18,300

River Transport
over the Centuries

Colleen Gahan

A Native American dugout.

An Egyptian riverboat.

Rivers have always been an important means of transport. For early humans, they were often the best way of transporting goods. Today, rivers are still important in our transport systems.

Early humans often settled along rivers where the soil was rich and there was a good water supply. They learnt to build rafts by tying logs together. These rafts were used to transport people and goods. Later, they built dugouts, a type of canoe which is made from hollowing out a log. Some Native Americans made boats by stretching animal hides over a wooden frame.

The ancient Egyptians were among the first great boat builders. They built huge barges (flat-bottomed boats) to carry heavy stone up the Nile River. The stone was used to construct their huge monuments. By 4000 BC, Egyptians were using reed riverboats powered by oarsmen. By about 3000 BC, they were building timber boats with sails.

Sailing ships were the main means of river transport, until the nineteenth century when steamboats were developed. In some countries, roads between some towns were poor or non-existent. Steamboats were very important; they carried people and produce between towns, or to the nearest port.

Before long, paddle steamers were being used along the rivers. During the mid-1800s, paddle steamers were used along rivers such as the Mississippi, Nile, Thames and the Murray.

Throughout history, barges have also been used. Sometimes they were towed by riverboats; sometimes they were powered by sails and sometimes they were pulled along by people walking along the river bank.

A barge.

If you visit a busy river today, you might see tug boats, barges, leisure craft, ferries and cargo ships all jockeying for position.

A paddle steamer.

The Legend of

Martin Pritchett

St George is the patron saint of England. He was born in the third century AD, but very little is known about his life.

The legend tells of a great, noble knight named George. According to the legend, he saved the king's land and its people from destruction, by defeating one of the fiercest dragons in all the land with a magic sword. The people were so astounded by George's bravery and victory over the dragon that over time, they declared him a saint.

After defeating the dragon, St George became a soldier and rose through the ranks to become a very high-ranking officer. He publicly followed his religious beliefs; a danger-ous thing to do in those times. He was arrested, tried and killed on 23 April 303 AD. St George's life is celebrated on this date.

St George

George's bravery and beliefs were greatly admired by the Crusaders, who were Christian soldiers that fought to recapture holy lands.

After the crusades, George was made the Patron Saint of England, and the red cross of St George was worn as a badge by English soldiers and still appears in the British Union Flag. This flag is incorporated into the designs of the flags of other nations, such as Australia, New Zealand, Fiji, Seychelles and St Helena.

How to Use a

A compass is an instrument you can use to find directions. Compasses are easy to use if you know how.

Let's take a look at how a compass works.

direction of travel arrow

compass needle

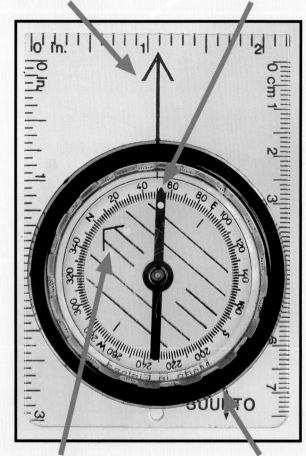

orienting arrow

compass housing

The first thing you need to find on a compass are the directions: north, south, east and west. North is the most important because the needle always points to this direction.

The red and black arrow is called the *compass needle*. The **red** part of it always points towards the earth's magnetic **north** pole.

The ring on the compass is called the *compass housing*. The compass housing ring moves, depending on the direction you need to go. Along the edge of the compass housing, you will find a scale from 0 to 360. These are called the degrees.

If you want to go in another direction you can combine two main compass points. For example, if you would like to go in a direction between north and east, you would move "north-east".

Compass

Moving in a North-East Direction

1. Find north-east on the compass housing. Turn the compass housing to north-east. Make sure that it faces the large **direction of travel arrow**.

2. Hold the compass flat in your hand. Then turn yourself, your hand and the entire compass until the compass needle is aligned with the orienting arrow inside the compass housing.

3. Time to check! It is important that the red or north part of the compass needle points at north in the compass housing. If the south part of the needle points at north, you would walk off in the opposite direction of where you want to go!

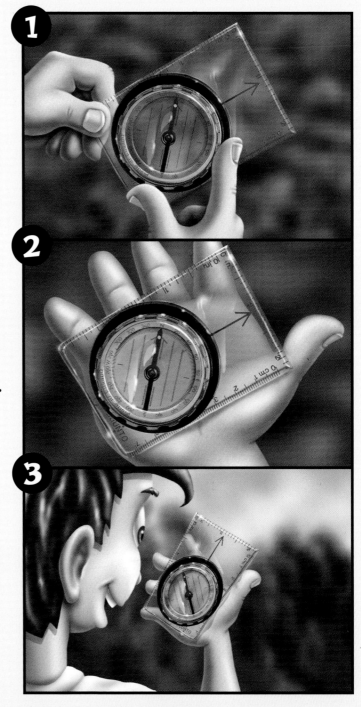

Encouraging Others

Helen McGrath and Toni Noble

We learn new things all the time. Some people say that they never stop learning! Here are some helpful tips to keep in mind when people are learning something new.

We all make mistakes when we're learning and improving. Show others that you understand!

- When someone gets something wrong or doesn't go well, remember how it felt when something like that happened to you.

- Don't point out their mistake or lack of improvement.

- Say something encouraging.

- Sometimes, a funny comment helps, but make sure you don't use humour to put the other person down.

- Remember that what they most want from you is *respect* and *understanding*.

- Sometimes, it helps to just touch them very lightly and quickly on the arm or shoulder to let them know that you understand.

- When they do master it, be positive but don't go overboard.

Look at the pictures below. This is what you might hear and notice when people are encouraging others.

You'll get it next time.

See how he's smiling.

You're nearly there.

See how she has friendly eyes.

This is hard, isn't it?

He is using a friendly voice.

I had trouble with this, too.

See how his body is relaxed.

Earthquake Drill

During an Earthquake

When you feel an earthquake, duck under a desk or a sturdy table. Stay away from windows, bookcases, filing cabinets, heavy mirrors, hanging plants and other heavy objects that could fall. Watch out for falling plaster and ceiling tiles. Stay undercover until the shaking stops and hold onto your cover. If it moves, move with it. Here are some additional tips for specific locations:

- If you are in a **high-rise building** and not near a desk or table, move against an interior wall and protect your head with your arms. Do not use the elevators. Do not be surprised if the alarm or sprinkler systems come on. Stay indoors. Glass windows can dislodge during the quake and sail for hundreds of metres.

- If you're **outdoors**, move to a clear area away from trees, signs, buildings, electrical wires and poles.

- If you're on a **footpath near buildings**, duck into a doorway to protect yourself from falling bricks, glass, plaster and other debris.

- If you're **driving**, pull over to the side of the road and stop. Avoid overpasses, power lines and other hazards. Stay inside the vehicle until the shaking is over.

- If you're in a **crowded store or other public place**, do not rush for the exits. Move away from display shelves containing objects that could fall.

- If you're in a **wheelchair**, stay in it. Move to cover if possible, lock your wheels and protect your head with your arms.

- If you're in the **kitchen**, move away from the refrigerator, stove and overhead cupboards.

- If you're in a **stadium or theatre**, stay in your seat and protect your head with your arms. Do not try to leave until the shaking is over, then leave in a calm, orderly manner. Avoid rushing towards the exits.

from the *Earthquake Preparedness Handbook*, Los Angeles City Fire Department

Rattles and Shakers

Noel and Phyllis Fiarotta

In many parts of the world, rattles and shakers have been used to accent the rhythm of a dance or song. Native Americans still use rattles as part of their ceremonial dances and chants.

Here is a rattle you can make from items you have at home.

You will need:

- a clean plastic bottle
- a wooden stick
- some rice
- left-over fabric
- Blu-Tack
- a craft knife
- ribbons, feathers and beads

1 Find a wooden stick that is about twice as long as the bottle. Check that the stick fits tightly into the neck of the bottle.

2 Cut a cross in the centre of the bottom of the bottle. Ask an adult to help you.

3 Pour some rice into the bottle.

4 Push the stick through the neck of the bottle, and out through the hole at the bottom.

5 Press Blu-Tack around each end of the stick to stop the rice falling out.

6 Cover the bottle with fabric and decorate your rattle. Tie ribbons around the stick and add feathers and beads.

Maze Madness

Colleen Gahan

I'd had a great time at the Fun Park, doing all sorts of interesting things, until somehow I found myself alone in the mirror maze. That's when things took a turn for the worse.

It was towards the end of the day and there weren't many people about. At first it was fun, looking at myself in the funny mirrors.

Sometimes I looked really tall and skinny as a beanstalk.

Next I would see myself,

fat and roly-poly, with a double chin and a big round, chubby face, and fingers like fat sausages.

I started pulling faces at the mirrors and standing in funny positions. I was really enjoying myself, until… suddenly I realised I couldn't hear any voices around me.

I was the only person left in the maze!

I couldn't find my way out. I kept walking up and down, but the exit had disappeared. I began to call out for Mum **and Dad,** **LOUDLY** but there was no reply! My hands were **hot** and **sweaty**, and my head was **throb**bing. I was close to tears. What if I never got out? What if the Fun Park closed with me still in the maze? I was beginning to feel desperate and all the time I kept walking—down and up, and up and down.

Just then I heard a **shout**. I called out as loudly as I could, and in an instant, Mum was there, leading me outside.

I was so relieved I **burst** into tears!

The River

JAMES CARTER

from a tiny spring the river came and
wound its
for way
days and
first days
east
then
but west
always
south
always
down
even
when it
c
r u
l
e
d
itself
a
r o
u n
d a
b
e n d
but
then
one day
something changed
and a river it could no longer be
for the river grew and the river knew that now it was

THE SEA THE SEA THE SEA THE SEA THE SEA THE SEA THE SEA
THE SEA THE SEA THE SEA THE SEA THE SEA THE SEA THE SEA
THE SEA THE SEA THE SEA THE SEA THE SEA THE SEA THE SEA
THE SEA THE SEA THE SEA THE SEA THE SEA THE SEA THE SEA
THE SEA THE SEA THE SEA THE SEA THE SEA THE SEA THE SEA
THE SEA THE SEA THE SEA THE SEA THE SEA THE SEA THE SEA

George's Feelings

Chris McTrustry

I keep telling myself to stay cool. Yeah, George. Be cool. But who can be cool when your hands are sweaty and your head feels like it's a balloon, light and full of air and ready to burst at any second?

Be cool, George.

Huh! I won't even think about what's going on in my stomach. But there must be butterflies the size of fighter jets crashing into one another down there!

I wish I had a fighter jet. Then I'd show Lance a thing or two. But I'd need a few jets, 'cause he's really tough—and BIG. I think I could handle "the situation" if he wasn't so BIG.

And that dog Puff… well, I reckon there are lions smaller than him—and less vicious!

But one day, I'll stand up to them. Yeah. I'll hassle them. Or… maybe I should just ask them, really nicely, to leave me alone. No more hassle.

After all, a kid can only take so much…

"That's My Boy!"

Jan Pritchett

Gilbert is part of the school soccer team but he doesn't always get a game. So when he is chosen to play in the final, he really wants to prove himself. Gilbert's mum was there to see the action. That night, she pens her thoughts in her diary.

Dear Diary,

I was delighted that I could help Gilbert's soccer team get to the final important game by supplying the substitute bus. As I drove my bus, I could hear that big-mouth kid Duncan giving my Gilbert a hard time. It took all my self-control not to give that bully a piece of my mind, but I knew that it wouldn't do Gilbert any good if I lost my temper.

I watched Gilbert's uncertainty when we arrived at the field. I could see that he thought he wouldn't get to play. And I knew he would be bitterly disappointed. My stomach was in a tight knot; I really felt for my boy. Then, the next thing I knew, he had found out that he would be playing.

My heart pounded whenever the ball came anywhere near Gilbert throughout the game. When the score was still a draw near the end of the game, the suspense was dreadful—you could cut the air with a knife. My mouth was dry and my palms were cold and clammy. Would the team blame Gilbert if they didn't win?

The match outcome was in Gilbert's hands or, actually, as it turned out, his head.

It was absolutely unbelievable the way he effortlessly put that ball into the net so the other team's goalkeeper couldn't reach it—he did it without even looking!

Everyone went wild. I was so proud! I had to blink repeatedly to stop the tears of relief and joy that I could feel pricking the back of my eyelids as I whispered, "That's my boy, Gilbert. That's my boy!"

Yaya

Yaya is the name given to a grandmother by children in Greece.

Though Sundays were special, Yaya still wore the same heavy, black Yaya-uniform that she wore every day: a black petticoat, a thick black dress, wrinkly black cotton stockings, scuffed black slipper-like shoes, and a black scarf coming down low on her brow and tied under her chin so that it completely covered the mass of long grey-white hair that was braided up beneath it.

Yaya was short, and she was fat in a solid, pyramid-shaped way, for she looked as most Cretan women have looked since the days when the Earth Mother ruled Crete and all men trembled at Her power.

* * * * *

One thing however that Yaya couldn't do was get the knack of speaking English.

from *Dancing in the Anzac Deli* by Nadia Wheatley